Dear In ith
Gres ✓ **W9-CZY-617**
you!!!
See you in
New Zealand
☺ Natasha

GUIDE

AUCKLAND WAR MEMORIAL MUSEUM

Te Papa Whakahiku

INTRODUCTION AND TEXT
Lucinda Blackley

PHOTOGRAPHY
Krzysztof Pfeiffer

Auckland**Museum**
Te Papa Whakahiku

AUCKLAND WAR MEMORIAL MUSEUM

Domain Drive, Auckland
Private Bag 92018
Auckland
New Zealand

Phone: (0064) 09 309 0443
Fax: (0064) 09 379 9956
Museum Store: (0064) 09 309 2580

store@akmuseum.org.nz
www.akmuseum.org.nz

First Published 2002
©Auckland War Memorial Museum 2002
Introduction and text by Lucinda Blackley
Photography by Krzysztof Pfeiffer,
except where indicated
Additional images ©Mark Klever,
Evan Reece and Haru Sameshima

The front cover photograph is of
Te Puawai o Te Arawa, the back flap
shows the shell of the *Paper Nautilus*

ISBN 0-908623-55-0

Design by Inhouse4.com
Printed in Hong Kong

WELCOME

Welcome to Auckland War Memorial Museum, where exciting stories of the Pacific, New Zealand's people, and the flora, fauna and landforms of our unique islands, are told within a memorial dedicated to those who have sacrificed their lives for our country.

In one of New Zealand's most outstanding historical buildings, boldly situated in the Domain – a central-city pleasure garden – you encounter exhibitions that will excite you with the artistic legacy and cultures of the peoples of the Pacific; the monumental carvings, buildings, canoes and taonga (treasures) of the Maori; and the diversity of cultures which now combine to form the rich tapestry of race, nationality and creed which is modern New Zealand.

You will enter a world of knowledge about the environment handed down to us by Maori and be dwarfed by the original inhabitants of this land, when, in the age of the dinosaurs, New Zealand split off from the great southern continent Gondwana. You will explore the coastal and mountain habitats of New Zealand and its ocean realms and be enchanted with the hands-on learning environments for children in our twin Discovery Centres. You will delve into rich information resources in our top-floor Library and its satellite information centres; 'The Armoury' and 'Matapuna'. You will trace our emergence as a uniquely different people in the tragic, heroic, but also proud stories of wartime endeavour told in the "Scars on the Heart" exhibition.

Auckland Museum is a vast treasure house, protecting and interpreting one-and-a-half centuries of collecting. Its collections are vast in scale, deep in quality and profound in their importance to our nation. They are also the exciting touchstones of our history and identity, putting you in touch with our origins. Around them our staff provide programmes of events and special exhibitions, special tours and other activities. Details of these pro-grammes are available in the Museum's arrival foyer, where you will also find located our café and, very special, Museum Store.

We hope that you will enjoy your visit, return and visit us again, be our ambassador carrying the reputation of this Museum far beyond our walls, and that this little book will be a souvenir of a memorable visit.

FROM THE COLLECTIONS: a feather cocktail dress by Auckland fashion designers Francis Hooper and Denise L'Estrange Corbet of *World*, 1997

Dr T L Rodney Wilson
Director

INTRODUCTION

TOP: The Museum in 1870, housed in the old Princes Street Post Office

RIGHT: The Institute and Museum building, Princes Street, 1917

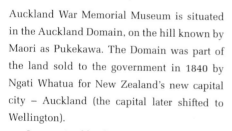

Auckland War Memorial Museum is situated in the Auckland Domain, on the hill known by Maori as Pukekawa. The Domain was part of the land sold to the government in 1840 by Ngati Whatua for New Zealand's new capital city – Auckland (the capital later shifted to Wellington).

In 1852 Auckland's first Museum, the oldest in the country, opened in a two-room farm cottage in Grafton Road - one room for the collection, one for the custodian's accommodation. Its collecting focus was Ethnology and Natural History. Relocating in 1867 and again in 1870, the Museum moved into its first custom-built premises, in Princes Street, in May 1876. The Museum collections continued to grow and, by the time of World War I, were again in desperate need of new premises.

The war had an enormous impact on New Zealand. 18,166 men were killed, from a total population of only one million. Nearly all those killed were buried overseas, and almost a third have no known grave. Families had nowhere to focus their grief and say goodbye to their loved ones. War memorials, acting as symbolic tombs for mourning families, were an important part of the national grieving process.

After the war ended in 1918, Auckland considered ways to commemorate its war dead, and after much discussion it was decided to combine the War Memorial for the Auckland Province with a world-class new Museum.

An international architectural competition, held to design the new building, was won by the Auckland firm Grierson, Aimer and Draffin in 1922. All three architects were veterans of the

TOP: Interior of the over-crowded Princes Street building, c 1890

BOTTOM: Preparator Mr LT Griffin at work in his Princes Street laboratory, c 1909

'Great War', fighting at either the Western Front or Gallipoli. Two of the three lost brothers.

Construction was funded by money raised by public subscription, particularly by the efforts of women wishing to mourn their loved ones and by returned servicemen wishing to honour their fallen comrades. Central government contributed a small portion.

Prime Minister J Gordon Coates laid the foundation stone in July 1925, and the official opening and consecration ceremony was held on 28 November 1929. The Maori opening ceremony the next day was attended by 80 rangatira (chiefs) from all over the Auckland region.

The solemnity of the neo-classical design was appropriate for the memorial function of

the building, underpinning values of valour and heroism. The architects sought to recreate the view of Greek temples that many servicemen had seen from the decks of warships in the Mediterranean. A small hill in front of the Museum was removed so that the building could be better seen from the Waitemata Harbour.

The Cenotaph (empty tomb) in front of the Museum is a replica of the Tomb of the Unknown Soldier in Whitehall, London. Attempts were made to purchase the original blueprints, but they proved too expensive. The architects sketched the monument from movie newsreels, and drew their own plans.

One of the most beautiful elements of the building is the frieze that runs around the top of the exterior of the building. Each picture depicts a scene from World War I, or on the extension to the building added thirty years later, World War II. Above each exterior window is the name of a battle in which New Zealand services fought. A poppy motif, symbol of the Returned Services Association (RSA), is found throughout the building. The Maori-influenced designs around the interior colonnades plant the Museum's roots firmly in Aotearoa New Zealand.

ABOVE: Stonemasons at work on the colonnade, 1920s

BELOW: The waka *Te Toki-a-Tapiri* is moved to its new home in the current Museum, c 1929

After World War II it was decided to expand the War Memorial to honour all of Auckland Province's fallen soldiers. The additions would include new Halls of Memory to remember the 11,671 men and women killed in World War II. (The names of those who fought in subsequent wars were added later).

Coinciding with the need to expand the Auckland War Memorial was the need to

increase the Museum's exhibition, storage and workspace. The extension added two thirds more floor space, improving the balance of storage and work areas. Fundraising began in 1946, with the extension opening in March 1960. The final addition, an auditorium, was officially opened in October 1969.

Auckland Museum has outstanding Natural History, Social History, Ethnology, Decorative Arts, Library and Pictorial resources in addition its Military collections. One of the Museum's great characters was Thomas Cheeseman, sole Curator of the Museum for almost 50 years (1874 – 1923), who saw the great expansion of the Ethnographic and Natural History collections from virtually nothing to world-renowned status. His directorship saw bequests by: Thomas Russell (antique statuary casts intended to form the basis of Auckland's first art school), James Tannock Mackelvie (who donated a wonderfully eclectic collection of art, ethnographic and historic pieces – a Museum gallery is devoted to his bequest), Gilbert Mair (whose ethnographic collection was first deposited in 1890 and later purchased by the Museum), Governor Sir George Grey (ethnology, archaeology, art and personal effects so evocative of the period when he dominated New Zealand history) and Sir John Logan Campbell, so-called 'Father of Auckland'. Cheeseman was the visionary behind the move to the Domain, but sadly died before it was completed.

Auckland Museum's collection of Maori taonga (treasures) is one of the greatest in the world, predominantly due to the generosity of Maori in sharing their taonga with all the peoples of Auckland.

TOP: The official opening of Auckland War Memorial Museum on the 28th November 1929

RIGHT: Auckland War Memorial Museum as seen from the Parnell foreshore, c 1929

BOTTOM: The Guard of Honour from St Stephens College is inspected at the 1929 opening

The Pacific artefacts are internationally renowned, with an outstanding collection of traditional and contemporary arts from all over the region, reflecting Auckland's place as the world's largest Polynesian city.

The Natural History collection is one of the four major research collections of the nation. Its large holdings of native and exotic birds were developed by early curators such as Cheeseman and Sir Gilbert Archey, who traded duplicates with museums around the world. Archey was largely responsible for the Museum's collection of moa bones.

The Applied Arts collection features not only New Zealand work but significant pieces from around the world, for example the Fenton collection of English pewter and the large collection of Asian ceramics. The Charles Edgar Disney Art Trust and the Mackelvie Trust continue to fund new acquisitions.

The collections continued to grow so that by the 1990s a tiny fraction of the Museum's holdings could be publicly displayed. By this time the building was also showing signs of old age. A massive structural re-strengthening programme was carried out; simultaneously, all galleries were redesigned and refitted. Completed in 1999, the new displays are object-rich, enabling more treasures to be publicly displayed than ever before. Prime Minister Helen Clark officially re-opened Auckland War Memorial Museum on 18 March 2000.

HE TAONGA MAORI

Maori are the indigenous people of Aotearoa New Zealand. Auckland Museum is of special significance to Maori on three very important levels. First and foremost, the Museum is established upon customary land (mana whenua) of Ngati Whatua O Orakei, the home tribe (tangata whenua) of Auckland. Secondly, it is a war memorial, a shrine (wahi tapu) to New Zealand's war dead, of whom many hundreds were Maori. And thirdly, the Museum is responsible for the care of the largest and most comprehensive collection of Maori treasures (taonga) in the world. Over 1000 taonga are displayed in the new Maori galleries, completed in the year 2000. The taonga in the Museum include ancestral representations of all the major tribes of Aotearoa. These ancient items, be they carved, woven or otherwise, provide descendants with tangible links to ancestral landscapes and associated events. They embody spiritual power measured in terms of mana (ancestral authority), tapu (restriction from everyday being) and korero (associated narratives), and continue to be viewed as key symbols of tribal identity by Maori today.

In keeping with the Museum's commitment to the Treaty of Waitangi, New Zealand's founding document, the Museum has sought to develop proactive Maori initiatives in all its operations. In 1996 the Taumata-a-Iwi (Maori Advisory Committee) was established under government legislation. This legislative provision for an indigenous people to contribute at governance level to a Museum is unprecedented in world terms. The Taumata-a-Iwi guides the Museum in its implementation of Maori values (kaupapa Maori). Under their guidance dedicated Maori positions were created to bring a new level of integration of Maori policy, practice and procedure in all aspects of Museum operations.

Paul Tapsell
Tumuaki Maori

HEI TIKI

Hei tiki are highly valued ornaments made from pounamu (New Zealand jade or greenstone). Worn by both men and women, they are passed down through generations as family heirlooms. Hei tiki gain mana (honour or prestige) from having been in such close contact with the ancestors who have worn them in the past, and may be given their own personal names.

Te Toki-a-Tapiri is the last of the great war canoes (waka taua); the 25 metre hull could carry over 50 warriors. Its illustrious history began around 1836 in the Hawkes Bay, when Ngati Kahungunu chief Te Waaka Tarakau commissioned its carving, naming it after his ancestor Tapiri. Before completion it was given to the Rongowhakaata people of Poverty Bay, whose artists completed the carving; Tarakau received a famous cloak in exchange. In 1853 the canoe was presented to the renowned Ngapuhi warrior chiefs Tamati Waka Nene and Patuone, to mark the end of their raids against the East Coast peoples. Te Toki-a-Tapiri was later sold to the Ngati Te Ata people of Waiuku, just to the south of Auckland. When war broke out in the Waikato between Crown and Maori in 1863, government forces seized the waka although Ngati Te Ata had not taken up arms - compensation was paid after the war. In 1865 the waka took pride of place in a regatta on the Waitemata Harbour celebrating the visit of Prince Alfred, Duke of Edinburgh. Auckland's Ngati Whatua people then cared for the waka until the government presented it to Auckland Museum in 1885.

ABOVE: Bow (tauihu) of Te Toki-a-Tapiri.

An elaborately carved pataka (raised store-house) was a symbol of a chief's mana, and designed to store preserved foods, weapons and other valuables. *Te Puawai o Te Arawa*, or the Flower of Te Arawa, was commissioned by famous Te Arawa leader Te Pokiha Taranui, and completed in the early 1870s at Maketu in the Bay of Plenty. The carved figures on the porch represent Te Pokiha's ancestors, illustrating his descent from Tama-te-Kapua (the large figure over the door) who led the Te Arawa canoe in its migration from the ancestral land of Hawaiiki to Aotearoa New Zealand.

RIGHT: Detail - *Te Puawai o Te Arawa.*

Decorated gourds (below), kept in pataka, were used to store birds preserved in their own fat. This taha huahua, from the Urewera district on the inland east coast of the North Island, is decorated with a carved mouthpiece, hawk feathers and plaited harakeke (flax).

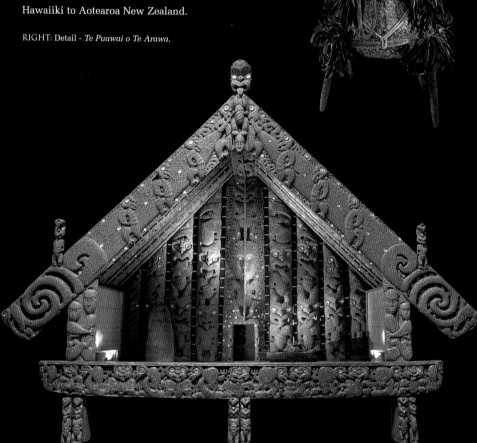

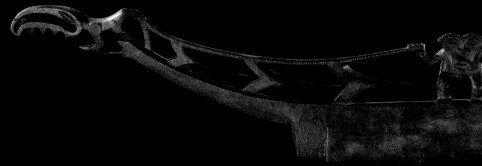

THE KAITAIA CARVING

The Kaitaia carving is often heralded as the artistic signpost linking Maori carvings with older Polynesian styles. Carved from totara, and thought to date from the 14th to 16th centuries (soon after Maori arrived in New Zealand), this taonga was found in a swamp near Kaitaia (Northland) in 1920. The angular forms distinguish this period of Maori carving from later curvilinear styles.

ARCHAIC JEWELLERY

This unusual pendant (right) was found near the Bay of Islands after a storm in 1895. The tiny human figures are reminiscent of East Polynesian art. The pendant is thought to date from soon after the arrival of Maori from Polynesia.

KAHU HURUHURU

Decorated with green and white feathers of the kereru (New Zealand pigeon), and with a border of red kaka feathers, this kahu huruhuru cloak (far right) is thought to be around 100 years old.

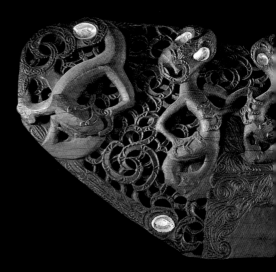

PARE FROM PATETONGA

The Patetonga pare (lintel) was probably carved in the early 19th century with stone tools, and is thought to represent Hine-nui-te-po (goddess of death) or Papatuanuku (earth mother) giving birth to the gods.

TUTANGIMAMAE

A whakawae (door jamb) from the house *Tutangimamae*, which stood near what is now Helensville, just north of Auckland. The house was carved by Te Ure of the Kawerau people in the mid 17th century.

IWIRAKAU

Famous carver, and ancestor of the Ngati Porou tribe, *Iwirakau* is depicted in this poutokomanawa (central post of a meeting house) from the east coast of the North Island.

TIKI

This kuwaha (gateway) is named *Tiki*, after a Ngati Whakaue ancestor. In the 1830s he guarded one of three entrances to Pukeroa pa (fortified village) at Ohinemutu, around which the city of Rotorua stands today. In 1889 *Tiki* was presented to the government and later placed in Auckland Museum. In the early 20th century the Museum coated him in red paint believing this offered a more 'authentic' representation of Maori carvings; in 1982 the process was reversed to reveal *Tiki's* original bright paint work as applied by Ngati Whakaue in the 1880s.

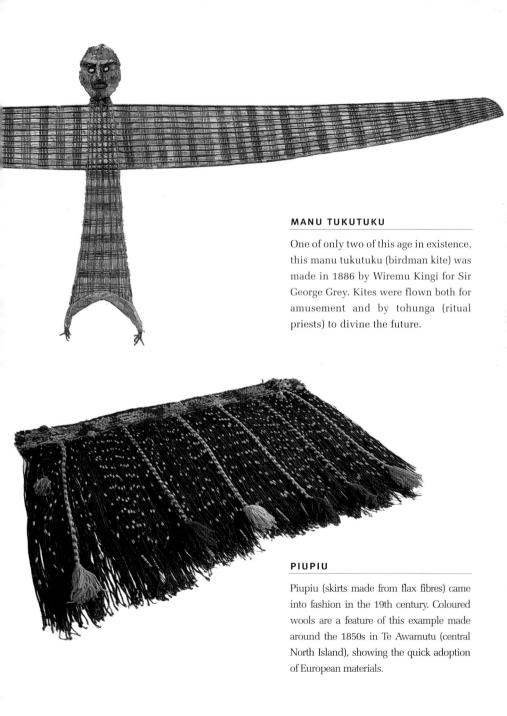

MANU TUKUTUKU

One of only two of this age in existence, this manu tukutuku (birdman kite) was made in 1886 by Wiremu Kingi for Sir George Grey. Kites were flown both for amusement and by tohunga (ritual priests) to divine the future.

PIUPIU

Piupiu (skirts made from flax fibres) came into fashion in the 19th century. Coloured wools are a feature of this example made around the 1850s in Te Awamutu (central North Island), showing the quick adoption of European materials.

PORTRAIT OF PATARA TE TUHI BY C F GOLDIE

Patara Te Tuhi, of the Ngati Mahuta people, was painted by C F Goldie in 1901. An advisor to the second Maori King, Tawhiao; he edited a Maori language newspaper in the 1860s. Although philosophically opposed to war against the Pakeha, he fought against the British Army during the Waikato Wars of 1863-64. Following their defeat, Patara accompanied King Tawhiao into seclusion in the King Country. In 1884 he journeyed with Tawhiao to England, where they petitioned Queen Victoria to limit the colonial government's sovereignty over Maori.

CARVED GUN

A gun carved and used by East Coast
Maori towards the end of the 19th century New Zealand Wars. A naturalistic
huia bird is depicted on one side.

KETE WHAKAIRO

Kete (baskets) are usually made out of
harakeke (New Zealand flax). Decorated kete
are highly valued for their character and
artistry. This example was donated by the Te
Kaha people to their local policeman, G A
McCurrah, when he retired in 1951.

PACIFIC PATHWAYS

Our Pacific collections are one of the most important in the world, and reflect New Zealand's place as a Pacific nation. In the *Lifeways Gallery* histories and cultures are explored; and in *Masterpieces* 600 treasures are displayed as art objects to emphasise their aesthetic beauty.

TIVAEVAE TAOREI

Introduced by missionaries, the craft of quilting was readily adopted by Pacific women and has evolved into the beautiful art-form known as tivaevae. Tivaevae have many ceremonial uses, such as being exchanged at weddings, presented to important visitors and used to adorn churches. This piece was designed and made by Mrs Kaitamaki of Aitutaki, Cook Islands, in 1969.

DAVENIYAQONA

Fijian priests used daveniyaqona (ritual
yaqona dish) like this for ceremonial purposes
within the spirit house (village temple).
Yaqona is the Fijian word for kava.

TONGAN GODDESS FIGURE

Around 1829 Tongan chief and Christian convert Taufa'ahau, who later became King George Tupou I, destroyed many images of Tongan gods during his country's transition from traditional religion to Christianity. One of only five figures of this type to survive worldwide, this goddess figure is thought to represent Hikule'o, Tongan goddess of the spirit world. Three of the five figures are held in Auckland Museum.

HIAPO BARKCLOTH OF NIUE

Hiapo, Niuean tapa, is cloth beaten from the bark of the paper mulberry tree. Tapa making is largely (but not exclusively) a female art, and is practised in many Pacific nations.

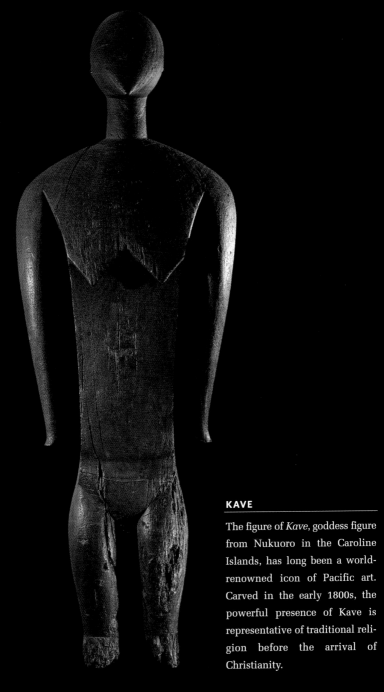

KAVE

The figure of *Kave*, goddess figure from Nukuoro in the Caroline Islands, has long been a world-renowned icon of Pacific art. Carved in the early 1800s, the powerful presence of Kave is representative of traditional religion before the arrival of Christianity.

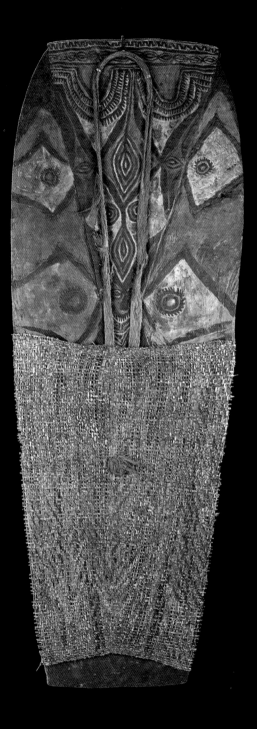

RAMU RIVER SHIELD

Papua New Guinean craftsmen give as much consideration to the decoration of shields as to practicalities such as size and weight. Some designs represent ancestors who it is hoped will protect the bearer, while other motifs either depict clan symbols or are designed to frighten the enemy. This example, from the Ramu River region, was made with stone tools in the early 20th century.

RA'IVAVAE GODDESS

Carved with amazing precision using stone tools, the designs on this Ra'ivavae goddess figure are typical of the Austral Islands.

RAKEITONGA, TIKOPIAN CANOE

This vaka tapu (sacred canoe) from Tikopia is called *Rakeitonga*, 'Over the East Wind', a name that refers to using the winds and sky for assistance on dangerous journeys. Built around 1900, this canoe was used for long distance voyages from Tikopia, and is one of the last few ocean-going canoes of this type in existence.

Photograph by Mark Klever.

EASTER ISLAND STONE HEAD

Few museums in the world house stone sculptures from Easter Island, as their size and weight made it difficult to transport them off the island during the heyday of museum collecting. This figure probably had stones inlaid in the eyes, perhaps obsidian for the pupil.

AHU'ULA FEATHER CLOAK, HAWAII

This Hawaiian feather cloak is called *ahu'ula*, meaning 'red garment'. Red was the colour associated with gods and chiefs throughout Polynesia; these cloaks were only worn by the highest ali'i (chiefs). Maori call a feather cloak made from high-status red kaka feathers *kahu kura*, which demonstrates the ancient Polynesian relationship in language and traditions.

MARADA DANCE MASK

A Marada mask used in rain-making rituals in the Tabar Islands off the Papua New Guinea coast. The broken stub in its mouth was probably part of a carved bird or lizard. Only five masks of this type are known to have survived worldwide - the last was carved decades ago.

BEADED APRON

The shell disks in this beaded apron from the Admiralty Islands, Papua New Guinea, are a traditional form of currency. Women wore these aprons at their weddings, and at feasts and dances, visibly displaying their family's wealth.

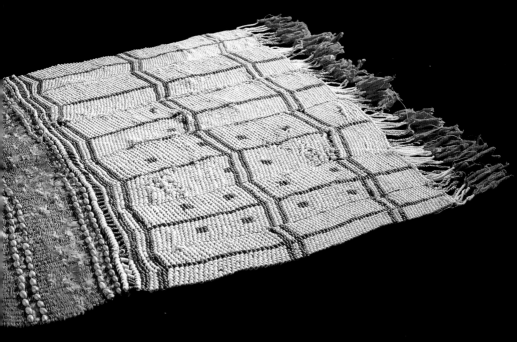

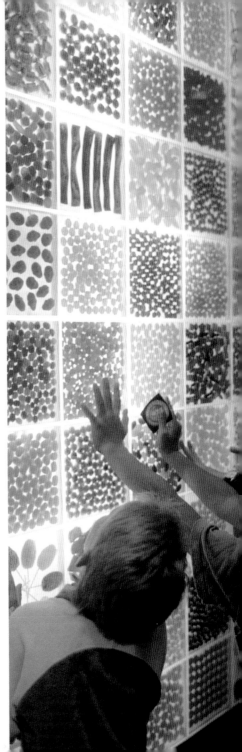

WILD CHILD

Wild Child explores the childhood experiences of Pakeha New Zealanders from the 19th century until the present day. Home life and school life are contrasted with the unstructured freedom and fantasy world of play.

TEDDY & JUMBO

These beloved toys were brought to New Zealand in the 1920s by sisters Fay and Tessa Mullet. Fay bequeathed them to the Museum on her death in 1992. Jumbo the elephant is a Steiff toy made in Germany about 1904, while Teddy is an English bear dating from around 1910.

SWEET WALL

Nostalgia for the sweet-toothed: favourite lollies from the corner dairy.

RAJAH THE ELEPHANT

Rajah has been an icon to Museum goers for generations. The original taxidermy, in the 1930s, took over a year to complete. Former Director Graham Turbott recalls that year: *"The whole museum smelled of elephant. No one will ever forget Rajah."* Rajah has recently been restored to his original glory.

CITY GALLERY

Some cities have been around for millennia. But in Auckland's case, the first English colonists were welcomed here by Ngati Whatua in only 1840. Two long lifetimes later Auckland joined the million-plus club. Almost one in three New Zealanders now live in Auckland. It is a place where history happened quickly.

WEDDING DRESS, 1860

This 1860 wedding dress wasn't made in impractical white but instead was economically designed for future wear as a best dress.

THE KIWI SHED

Sometimes called the 'blokes museum', the garden shed is the repository of 'things which might come in handy one day'. Parked in the shed is a Morris Minor 1000, a popular choice on New Zealand roads in the 1950s and 60s.

COLONIAL IRON

19th century housework required considerable strength and endurance. This three kilogram charcoal iron is one example of the heavy equipment women needed to maintain the fastidiously well-groomed appearance required by respectable Victorian society.

THE AGE OF TELEVISION

The way New Zealanders see themselves has always been reflected and influenced by the media. In this gallery we see and hear major events from the 1920s to the 1990s as they were portrayed on radio, film and television.

DECORATIVE ARTS

Auckland Museum holds a wide range of the finest examples of national and international decorative arts, from ceramics to pewter, glass to furniture, musical instruments to fashion and clocks. The collection is displayed in both permanent and temporary shows, and a strong programme of exhibitions by historical and contemporary artists.

JEWELLERY BY ARETA WILKINSON

This series of brooches, by Ngai Tahu artist Areta Wilkinson from her *05 series* (1996), form a traditional Maori taniko pattern.

Photograph by Haru Sameshima.

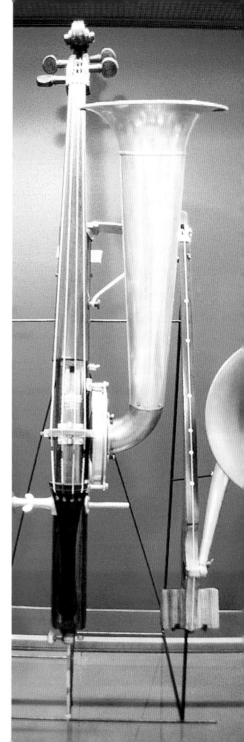

THE CASTLE COLLECTION

An eclectic collection of over 480 unique, rare and unusual musical instruments, the *Castle Collection* was the life passion of brother and sister Zillah and Ronald Castle. The diversity of the collection stretches from the very precious, such as an exquisite Klotz violin, to a mass-produced pitch pipe.

GLASS BY DALE CHIHULY

Sevres Blue and Gold Persian Set with Red Lip Wrap, by leading American glass artist Dale Chihuly, 1995.

FURNITURE BY GARTH CHESTER

Designed in 1947, this Garth Chester *curvesse chair* is widely considered to be one of the most significant pieces of furniture designed and made in New Zealand. The chair is formed from a single piece of ply, and is a local response to the international modernist movement.

ANCIENT
CIVILISATIONS

Civilisations takes us on a journey back through time to the world's first great cities. Their achievements in political systems, science and technology, philosophy and art form the basis of our modern world. Here, the ancient cultures of Egypt, Greece, Rome, China, Korea, Persia, Mesopotamia, and the Americas are represented by objects precious for their age, significance and beauty.

GREEK VASE

This hydria (water container) was made in Greece around 525 – 520 BC, the height of the classical period. The scene shows the *Judgement of Paris*, who, according to Greek mythology, had to decide who was the most beautiful goddess: Hera, Athena or Aphrodite (shown right to left). Also depicted is Hermes the messenger god – Paris stands next to him, holding a lyre.

GANDHARA BUDDHA

This Buddha was carved around 200- 300 AD in Gandhara, now northern Pakistan / east Afghanistan. Conquered by Alexander the Great in 27 - 26 BC, local artists came under the influence of Hellenistic traditions, and carvings from this period show many similarities to classical Greek sculpture. The Gandhara Buddha is of similar geographical origin to the monumental Bamiyan Buddhas.

GOLDEN FROG

Crafted in Panama between 900 and 1200 AD, this pre-Columbian golden frog was presented to Auckland city by Governor Sir George Grey. An unsuccessful attempt was made to steal the frog in 2001; the burglars snatched a worthless replica.

MUMMY PORTRAIT

During the Roman period of rule in ancient Egypt, wealthy citizens commissioned naturalistic painted portraits and used them as funerary masks for their mummies. This woman probably lived in the second or third century AD.

MUMMY

Egyptians believed that the body must be preserved after death in order for the soul to enjoy an afterlife. This young person died in the sixth or seventh century BC.

Maori cosmology.

TE AO TUROA

Te Ao Turoa (the Maori Natural History Gallery) celebrates the Maori view of the world. Traditional knowledge and explanations for the natural world, in the form of whakapapa (genealogies showing descent from the gods) and traditional stories, are featured alongside Maori scientific and technical knowledge.

TAUMATA ATUA

This stone image is a taumata atua (resting place of a god) and represents Rongo, the atua (spirit) of cultivated food crops. He is said to take up residence within it. When placed in a garden he ensured the fertility of the crop.

POU

Three pou (ancestral carved posts) represent the Maori tribes of Auckland: Ngati Whatua O Orakei (left), Tainui (centre) and Ngati Paoa (right). The Ngati Paoa pou is a unique example of modern carving. Commissioned for the Museum's relaunch in 2000, artist Tu Karamaene used only stone tools, which were in turn made using only traditional materials.

ORIGINS

Telling the stories of both our geological origins – how New Zealand split from the supercontinent Gondwana – and the origins of our unique plant and animal life, *Origins Gallery* takes us on a journey back through time, beginning when reptiles ruled. Here we explore why some of our birds and insects grew to an enormous size and many birds developed unusual traits such as flightlessness.

TUATARA

Tuatara are sometimes called 'living fossils' because they have survived for 200 million years virtually unchanged. Although they look like lizards they are not; their closest relatives died out at least 60 million years ago.

NEW ZEALAND DINOSAURS

Marine reptiles were long known to have lived during the Mesozoic era in the seas around what became New Zealand, but it wasn't until 1975 that amateur palaeontologist Joan Wiffen discovered fossilised remains of true dinosaurs and flying pterosaurs. New Zealand's tortured volcanic landscape has meant that few dinosaur remains have been preserved.

THE GIANT MOA

At three metres high, the giant moa was the tallest bird that ever lived; its egg had a volume of almost four litres. Ten other smaller species of moa existed, some only as big as a turkey. Moas filled the ecological niche that deer and other browsing animals took in other parts of the world.

HEAVY-FOOTED MOA

The bones of this heavy-footed species of moa were found in Canterbury.

LAND

New Zealand's landscape is one of drama and contrast, from snowy peaks to active volcanoes, limestone caves to lush sub-tropical rainforest, sandy white beaches to mangrove swamps. The *Land Gallery* presents a journey from mountain to coastline, revealing the plants, fungi, birds, reptiles and freshwater fish that make their home in our 'land of birds'.

BROWN KIWI

The kiwi is so unusual a bird that when the first specimen reached Europe it was considered a hoax. It is the only bird to have nostrils at the tip of its beak, it cannot fly and lays an egg that weighs one fifth of the female's body weight. Brown kiwi (*Apteryx australis*), the most common species, were once widespread throughout all three main islands but are now endangered.

Photograph by Mark Klever.

NIKAU

The nikau is the world's southernmost palm. Like many indigenous plants, the nikau is dependent on the kereru (New Zealand pigeon) to spread its seeds. The kereru is one of few surviving native birds able capable of swallowing the nikau's fleshy fruit.

WETA

The large tusked weta is a harmless, flightless cricket which has changed little since the Mesozoic era. Its relative the giant weta, one of the world's heaviest insects, can weigh up to 50 grams. Nine of the eleven species of giant weta are endangered.

OCEANS

New Zealand is an island nation surrounded by coastline, home to many beautiful and unusual marine animals.

WALK-ON ROCK POOL

A walk-on, glass-covered, living rock pool offers a glimpse of some of the different kinds of animals that live along our rocky coastlines. Creatures such as crayfish, crabs and anemones live here together, although not always in harmony.

Photograph by Mark Klever.

PORCUPINE FISH

A Museum Educator points out to young visitors the fascinating porcupine fish (*Allomycterus jaculiferus*), which protects itself with tiny, hidden spines deeply set in the pores of its thick, leathery skin. When the fish becomes alarmed it puffs itself up like a balloon, with all its spines visible and fully extended.

The Poor Knights Islands, remnants of extinct volcanoes off New Zealand's northern east coast, are a unique ecological location that provides for a profusion of plant, sponge, coral, shell and fish life.

Photograph by Evan Reece

PAPER NAUTILUS

The female cuttlefish (a relative of the octopus), makes the paper nautilus (*Argonauta nodosa* or pupu terakihi in Maori) as an egg case and nursery for her young. She holds on to it with her two dorsal arms, leaving six arms for swimming and catching food. When the eggs hatch, the female dies, releasing the shell. This specimen, one of the largest ever collected, was found at Kaipara North Head.

PAUA

Known overseas as abalone, paua (*Haliotis spp.*) are marine snails related to clams, oysters, mussels and squids. They breathe by drawing water under the edge of the shell, and then over the gills and out the holes. Iridescent paua shell is often used for jewellery and ornaments, and the meat is a popular food.

KINA

A favourite kai moana (sea food) for many New Zealanders, kina (*Evechinus chloroticus*) use their spines for protection, feeding and movement. These sea urchins are members of a large group of marine animals that include sea stars and sea cucumbers.

CIRCULAR SAW SHELLS

The rare circular saw shell (*Astraea heliotropium*) was highly sought after by Victorian collectors, who named it after the Ancient Greek goddess of justice, star maiden Astraea.

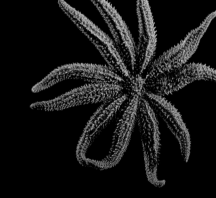

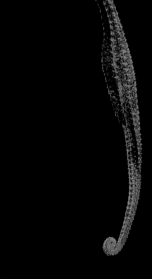

SEA STAR

Coscinasterias calamaria is a common shoreline sea star that can have as many as eleven arms. It has a voracious appetite, grows quickly, moves fast and eats kina, oysters and other shellfish.

SPINY SEADRAGON

A relative of pipefish and seahorses, spiny seadragons (*Solegnathus spinosissimus*) can be recognised by their coiled tails, long slender snouts and thin extended bodies, which are encased in spiny, ring-like plates. Males have been seen carrying eggs underneath their tails.

HUMAN IMPACTS

When Polynesians reached New Zealand about 1,000 years ago they found a land that had been physically isolated for some 80 million years. *Human Impacts* and *Matapuna Resource Centre* show the often negative effects people have wrought on our delicate eco-systems, yet offer hope for the future by educating a new generation to respect our environment.

ARK OF DESTRUCTION

When humans arrived in New Zealand so did land mammals, many extremely destructive for the environment. This display of introduced mammals shows them in order of arrival into New Zealand. All have had a severe impact on native plants and animals through predation, competition for food and browsing the forests. Introduced plants, fish and insects have wreaked similar destruction.

TINNED TOHEROA SOUP, CA 1960S

The toheroa is a large, burrowing shell-fish and a popular traditional food. But private and commercial over-harvesting has meant that the toheroa is now an endangered species. Today it is protected by law, but is still taken illegally.

CAESAR THE WONDER-DOG

Austrian hunter and taxidermist Andreas Reischek (1845 – 1902) spent twelve years in New Zealand shooting and collecting native birds. His specimens, some of species now extinct, can be found in museums around the world. This skull is that of his Newfoundland-Retriever 'Caesar', who was nick-named the 'wonder dog' for his 'astonishing feats of obedience and intelligence'.

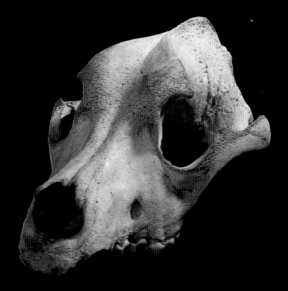

HUIA

Stuffed huia in bell jars were a popular display in Victorian living rooms, and study skins like these were sold to museums and collectors around the world. The huia was last sighted in 1907, and is now extinct.

THE LIBRARY

The Auckland Museum Library *Te Pātaka Mātāpuna* houses one of New Zealand's largest collections of heritage material, manuscripts and archives, photographs, paintings and drawings. *The Library* is in constant use by researchers, scholars and genealogists.

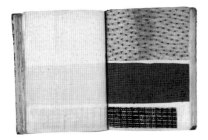

BOOK OF TAPA COLLECTED DURING CAPTAIN COOK'S VOYAGES

In 1787 Alexander Shaw, of London, compiled and published this book of tapa samples collected on the three Pacific voyages of Captain James Cook. Most of the pieces are from Hawaii, with others from the Society Islands, Tonga and Rurutu. Now over 200 years old, these are some of the oldest surviving pieces of tapa in the world. Only 30 copies of the book still exist.

CHILDREN'S
DISCOVERY CENTRE

Auckland Museum's award winning Children's Discovery Centre comprises two parts: *Weird & Wonderful* and *Treasures & Tales*. The first of its kind in New Zealand, the Centre continuously aims to set new standards for hands-on learning within an eclectic, exciting environment.

WEIRD AND WONDERFUL

From crawling tarantulas to volcanoes and oceans, and a working bee-hive smelling of fresh honey, *Weird and Wonderful* brings to life the colourful worlds of natural history. Tactile fun, learning and inspiration for the child inside all of us.

TREASURES AND TALES

Social history and cultural diversity are the focus of *Treasures and Tales*. Food, music, tools, medicine and clothing –from around the world and back in time– are explored with everything from dress-ups to drums to live rats.

HENARE TARATOA

NEW ZEALAND WARS

The New Zealand Wars, 1845–1872, were fought throughout the North Island between European settlers (backed by the British Army) and indigenous Maori tribes. Legislation finally defeated the struggle by Maori to retain possession and control over their land. In this gallery we tell the stories of both sides of the conflict.

HENARE TARATOA

Lay preacher Henare Taratoa insp[ired] Maori men and women to leave safety of a besieged pa (fort) at nig[ht] give water to wounded enemy lyin[g] the field of battle. Taratoa was kille[d] battle at Te Ranga; in his shirt po[cket] was found a quotation from the [B]ible reading "If thine enemy hunger, [feed] him. If he thirsts, give him dri[nk]" This image is from a watercolou[r by] Horatio Robley.

PATITI

Maori used patiti (a hand axe or toma-hawk) very effectively in close combat. This patiti belonged to Eruera Peka Makarini, also known as Baker McLean. Righthand man to guerrilla leader Te Kooti, he often used this weapon when carrying out executions.

RANGIRIRI BUGLE

A bugle blown at Rangiriri, a dec[isive] battle in the Waikato in 1863. Casua[lties] were heavy on both sides, and incl[uded] Maori women and children.

ANGLO-BOER WAR

As a young colonial nation New Zealand was anxious to prove its worth to Mother England, immediately volunteering to join the Empire's war of expansion in South Africa. Jingoism gripped the country, and town halls like this were the scene of fundraising fervour during the Anglo-Boer War (1899-1902).

THE ZEERUST CUP, 1901

This trophy commemorates what is believed to be New Zealand's first ever representative rugby league match, played in Zeerust, South Africa, by members of the No 11 (Auckland) Company of the New Zealand Mounted Rifles in 1901. Friendly sporting matches have always been a favourite pastime of our off-duty troops when serving overseas.

ZEALANDIA

A patriotic monument to the fallen, representing the then-popular national symbol 'Zealandia'. Zealandia was a daughter of 'Britannia', and represented our umbilical links to the British Empire before our growth as an independent nation.

WORLD WAR I

New Zealand sent more men to fight in World War I, per head of population, than any other nation. 18,166 New Zealanders died, from a country of only one million.

CAMEL SADDLE

During the Sinai campaign, camels were used not only for transporting food and supplies to frontline troops, but also as cavalry and field ambulances. The Imperial Camel Corps was famed for its mobility and skill in desert warfare.

Of the 8,556 New Zealanders who served in the Gallipoli campaign, 2,721 were killed and 4,752 wounded - some more than once. This image (left) shows the New Zealand dressing station on the beach at Anzac Cove, 1915. The photographer was field doctor Lt-Col Dr Percival Fenwick; in addition to his photographic collection, the Museum also holds his diary.

THE SANCTUARY

Almost a third of those killed have no known grave. Here the Auckland Roll of Honour is inscribed on the walls of the Museum, a memorial to commemorate the fallen.

4.5 INCH HOWITZER

A 4.5-inch Howitzer, as used by Anzac forces first at Gallipoli, and later on the Western Front.

WORLD WAR II

New Zealand was caught in the winds of the World War II, which swept the globe in 1939. Our forces fought in the skies, oceans and lands of the Pacific, Asia, Africa, and Europe. 11,671 New Zealanders were killed, and life was changed irrevocably for those left at home.

PERSONAL EFFECTS OF BILL COLEMAN

Fathers, sons and husbands left home to fight in Europe – many never returned. Ann Vogel donated these family mementos of her father Bill Coleman, who died, like so many other Kiwis, at El Alamein. Bill carried photos of his wife and daughter into battle; Ann was only four when he was killed.

HALL OF MEMORIES

The names of the men and women of Auckland killed during World War II are recorded in marble in the Hall of Memories. Panels commemorating New Zealand's losses in Korea, the Malaya-Borneo conflict and Vietnam are also enshrined here.

MITSUBISHI ZERO

This Japanese warbird, the Mitsubishi A6M3 Zero-sen 22, was damaged and rebuilt during the last few months of World War II, which ended before it could fly its final mission. The kamikaze pilot's task was to crash into the target, causing great damage to the enemy and certain death to himself.

"In April 1945 falling flowers of cherry trees seemed to symbolise the fate of young pilots".

–Nobuya Kinase
World War II Kamikazi instructor.

HIROSHIMA GLASSES

A pair of spectacles from Hiroshima, melted by the power of the world's first nuclear bomb attack.

FIELD TELEPHONE

A German-made field telephone, cutting edge technology in the 1940s.

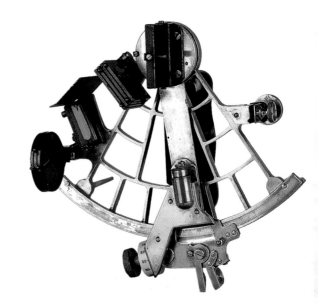

JAPANESE SEXTANT

This sextant was used on the Japanese submarine l-1, which was attacked by the New Zealand minesweepers *Kiwi* and *Moa* in January 1943 off the northwest coast of Guadalcanal. Despite being half its size, the *Kiwi* rammed the submarine three times – the Royal New Zealand Navy was eventually victorious.

REMEMBRANCE

George Lawson joined the Merchant Navy in 1943, and served in the North Atlantic. He stands next to the stained glass window which commemorates World War II naval sacrifices. Like many members of the Royal New Zealand Returned Services Association, he volunteers in the Armoury Resource Centre, sharing his knowledge and experiences with visitors and students.

Photograph by Evan Reece.

THE ARMOURY

The *Armoury* is a research centre which provides information about New Zealand's war history and the men and women who served and died. It also displays military items of historical importance from around the world.

CHARLTON GUN

In 1943 Mr Philip Charlton succeeded in converting a long magazine Lee Enfield to fire automatically. Women workers at Charlton's Hastings factory converted 2,000 Lee Enfields for use by the New Zealand Home Guard. This is one of only five Charltons known to have survived.

MEDALS

The United Nation's Korea Medal 1950-53 (above left) and the Vietnam Medal 1964, both awarded to Kiwi soldiers. Many New Zealand volunteers served in these conflicts.

PICTORIAL
COLLECTIONS

Auckland Museum holds one of the nation's most important pictorial collections – a wealth of historic paintings, rare watercolours, photographs and other artworks. Most of New Zealand's greatest photographers are represented here, while amateur albums of family snaps and soldiers' mementos are a hidden treasure for descendants and social historians.

SIR EDMUND HILLARY

In 1953, New Zealand hero Sir Edmund Hillary and Sherpa Tensing Norgay became the first men to reach the summit of Mt Everest. Hillary was also the first person since Scott in 1912 to travel overland from Antarctica's Scott Base to the South Pole (1958). He led the first ascent of Antarctica's Mt Herschel (1967) and served as High Commissioner to India (1985-1989). Sir Edmund and Lady Hillary were founding patrons of the Auckland War Memorial Museum Circle, an organisation of Museum supporters. This portrait (detail shown) by Edward Halliday was commissioned by Auckland mayor Sir Ernest Davis, and presented to the citizens of Auckland in 1955 to commemorate Hillary's remarkable achievement on Mt Everest.

THE ROBIN MORRISON COLLECTION

One of New Zealand's most loved photographers, Robin Morrison and his family donated his life work to Auckland Museum shortly before his death in 1993. Robin Morrison was well known for his sympathetic character studies; in *Norm Smith with his pet sheep Pebbles* (1979) he treats his subject with affection and dignity.